Celine Maria is a young woman who lives in the Netherlands with her partner. She spent her childhood moving around countries falling in love with – and escaping into – fairy tales, on-and off-screen heartthrobs and writing her little heart out. Most of her days are spent dreaming away in a world that keeps on spinning and that's perfectly fine by her.

There's method in my madness
  – Lauren Aquilina

Celine Maria

My Love Is Mine

Austin Macauley Publishers

Copyright © Celine Maria 2025

The right of Celine Maria to be identified as author of this work has been asserted by the author in accordance with sections 77 and 78 of the Copyright, Designs and Patents Act 1988.

All rights reserved. No part of this publication may be reproduced, stored in a retrieval system, or transmitted in any form or by any means, electronic, mechanical, photocopying, recording, or otherwise, without the prior permission of the publishers.

Any person who commits any unauthorised act in relation to this publication may be liable to criminal prosecution and civil claims for damages.

A CIP catalogue record for this title is available from the British Library.

ISBN 9781035814879 (Paperback)
ISBN 9781035814886 (ePub e book)

www.austinmacauley.com

First Published 2025
Austin Macauley Publishers Ltd®
1 Canada Square
Canary Wharf
London
E14 5AA

Writing and imagining magic have been a part of me for so long. However, these pages of poetry commenced when I was 15. Truly, they began as a young teenager trying to escape. Somehow, they eclipsed to one of the most pivotal parts of my being.

And so, I would like to thank a few people who were with me whilst writing this tale.

First, my parents for being so extraordinary that I could never be too crazy. Me being able to express my feelings makes you my opposites but mainly I am so much like you. So, through everything I am grateful that you fought to give me life.

Secondly, my brother and sister. You also fought for me, be it your own demons or those of others. Ultimately, you both nurtured the child and diva in me, and it means the world to me.

Thirdly, my friend. You remain my partner in discourse. You lit the spark I always had for writing and your belief in me is warming. You know who you are, and you mean the absolute world to me.

Lastly, my partner. Who you allow me to be makes you my muse. So again, I will forever be grateful. All my desires and everything I have always believed in, somehow centers around us. Let's keep figuring it all out, at the edge of nights.

Table of Contents

To Be Completely Honest with You,	**11**
Let It Commence	**13**
Twilight Dusk and Gloom	**31**
Fuck I Love You	**45**
My Heart Thrives in the Dark	**65**
Irrevocable Strength	**79**

To Be Completely Honest with You,

The following pages of words
are thoughts I uttered
mostly between 11 and 4 at night,
sometimes after a lot of wine,
and some were written on a screen
in a different continent when I was lonely and amazed but still confused, possibly even utterly lost about where I was in life and who I have always been.
But I have big thoughts and little actions,
and the following lines are just combusting riddles in my mind. And if you like,
I would love to share them with you.
They make little sense at times,
and they are far from logical and in no way a proper sequence, but they are my most prized personal possession.
They bring me to tears and laughter at any moment in life, and I hope that perhaps you might find a part of yourself in any one of them. Anyhow, to me
they are just proof that I might be so sane that I can only think of the insane, or perhaps I am so proudly deranged that I frenzy in this way. Who knows? But at this age… apparently, this is who I was meant to be.

Let It Commence

Light Me Up

When I was fifteen my heart first lit up. All-consuming and all stupefied.

I closed my eyes, and from the inside my skin crept with trembles. What I imagined was now turning into reality, and the wonder truly began.

I experienced euphoria by chasing womanhood through recklessness and bravery. In scavenging everything during fiery nights, even if they were sometimes lonely.

But then I turned a little older and people ate my heart out a little more.

So, I realized that coming of age doesn't just break your heart – it ravages your will to exist.

Because, whilst friends held me, and family guided me – some of them ultimately ruined me.

And yet I found redemption in a lover who lets me out of my body and transcends me above all.
But *love* at its best is many sided, and *anger* is so much more, capable of mastering sorrow above sensibility.

And when the two consummate together you are all
consumed by pain, despair, and exhilaration.
In search for partnership, for sex and retribution, for dreams,
for power, and above all else, for life.

So, you let yourself wreck over ruthless waves
and crash into towering ivory,
sinking more and more debris into frigid ebony depths.

But I kept whispering pretty words into my ears;
kept writing erratically onto each piece of my membrane
and in the end – above all else – I bewitched myself.

Now I'm twenty-two and finally on the verge
of understanding the power in possessing my love.

And in the exhilarating madness of persisting, –
I wrote an ode to Celine.

Odd

They say I often speak
But do not say anything
Which is odd
When my existence bursts with words
And I find incomparable beauty in them
More than in myself

A Tiny Taste of Life

When I first kissed those lips

And felt the soft promise they could give

I opened my eyes to realize

I just got a tiny taste of what a life together could be like

Beneath Floating Leafs

Somewhere there is a tree
and childishly our initials
are carved along a heart in dwindles

And somewhere beneath floating leaves
you truly gave yourself over to me
letting just sweetness cover what was stolen from you

And only we know where in that forest
we became such fools that we couldn't help falling into each other

The only thing that makes that memory less honeyed
is that both of us didn't realize yet
what a complete psycho I am
and what the years would slowly teach us
our bodies crave to utterly devour

Race Me

While exposing my neck

Your mouth devours my skin

Pulse after pulse streams through the vein you suck

Down to the centre of my being

Where you are restless and young

Faster and harder

Rougher and closer

Love me more, I plead?

Outrage Takes Over

Isn't it outrageous
How I want you to make me feel ravenous
And are we not a force of rage
That sweeps through the outskirts
Casted into the cold like a pair of outlaws

Byzantine Empire

Eastern romance
Somewhere along the hot south
I've got this bed along the water
Burning up in and out
Sun upon my skin
Feels sparking from my heart to thighs.

I've waited most of my young life to be adored like this
Got all these curves along my body
Dips and twists along the lines of growth
And with you along me, I can never wait to show them
With only you watching me.

Breaths heaving up and down
Legs move forward and forward
You make my heart so strong
Can't even be bothered by all the other shit I go through.

Kicking back with my eyes locked on you
Can't do anything but daydream in a place like this
Gosh this must be the life.
And as high as I feel, I need you to go low
In my head I play a sequence of all thousand nights you put me in heat
And I need it again until I fade out of consciousness
Pounding and pumping love through me
breaking every bloodstream until I'm senseless.

Now all I see are star signs.
There's still this tension between us
And we'd be fools if we ever forgot how blessed we must be

To smile together and feel nothing but love endlessly
It's not even something I can explain
But this thing we have is too good for me to feel like I even exist sometimes

Something I still just can't fucking grasp
So we better make this cyclical trace last.

Places

Lie down and let yourself be forsaken

To my tender and strong rhythm

So, you watch yourself disappear into your utmost desire

This fire.

And get lost in the only place you can find me.

I Long for You

I long for you
Though I have your heart
Your mind
Perhaps even the movement of your hands
I still long for you

I play these memories back in slow motion
Creating a different film in my thoughts for every state I put
myself through
And then awakened I attempt to sleep

Restless I pass the line into the reality of my sane imagination

Suitcases dropped on the floor
Shoes scattered across the room
Coats hung half over the chairs
Our breaths shifting the air in the room
Anticipating the expression of joy on your face
Before you give me all your love
And we say goodbye to everything beyond that door
In a simple embrace

I long for those memories
To live life through them with you
Again, and again
And that will be my garden of Eden
To follow you, to be friends with you in the afterlife

I'd give a part of my soul
To not be lost in my head and feel completely and truly the sun on my face as the strangers fade away
Your legs between mine
Your head on my shoulder and your chest in my arms
My world in my grasp and the earth beneath me
Crushed by so much love that it is like a ruthless pain I have never known
The universe to me in a perfect balance

Along the lines of my sanity
You carry the weight of my safe haven
For I will be lost in our memories
And you, just like them, I will never escape.

Slow Me Down
(because I want to get hitched)

Make me dream
Tonight, let me enlighten
Remind me why we walk this line
When all I want is to run

Slow me down
Let the breath of your voice cover my ear
Embrace me so my wings are set free
Where I can soar with colours flashing by me

Give me devotion
Even more than hurtful desire
In that silence, breathe me
Stop this race within me
At least for now as we let the story begin

Heathens

Just want to make it clear to you
What I want you to put me through
And there's no danger left with you
Yet it's still lethal to see this through

Baby can't you feel I'm so eager
To be brutalized by such a teaser
Look down at me so sure
Knowing you're the only cure

In about 10 seconds I'll be drinking
While your hands are sinking
Better hush me with your mouth
Before I'm screaming like a storm in drought

If I do it for you over and over again
And I leave no form of constrain
Can we do this even harder
While neither of us remain sane?

Unleash this chain
Let me earn a bit more pain
Will you test my limits?
And see what I inhibit?

Show me I know you baby
Let's *make* each other crazy
Just healing and dreaming
Like heathens that need to be breathing

For Evermore

I know it.

Down to the cores of my bones.

That you and I.

Will be for evermore.

Twilight Dusk and Gloom

Terrible Choices

Lovers make terrible choices,
so ready to destroy lives in the face of any type of dissatisfaction.
And if that is what either of us choose, I'll gladly watch the fire we started burn all that we have to the ground

– from ashes to nothing –
just to somehow build it up again because we will never have another place to run to.

There's no longer an escape no matter how brazen our spirits, so we might as well just imperialize it all and wear our crowns ready for battle.

Fighting until everything but us fades from this blessed existence.

Did You Have To?

Where the two rivers end
And slowly meet
Do you see what I see?

It's me beside you
Finally pronounced as two
If only you could believe

And would not rot away
Like the branches that reach out
From a long ancient tree

Fuck You or Maybe Me?

Do you forget who I am?
I know it's a sweet smile at first
A soft voice and a misleading touch
That's my bad
So, boy, I'm sorry
But now you know

My emotions take up a whole lot of space
My temper goes on even more rollercoasters
Fuck, I know I take it way too far more often than not

Will never raise my voice to scream or shout
Might just whisper your name to the lady above when
you're moving in and out

But when you're not holding my chest in your arms, so
solid and protected
You can bet my eyes will kill
My hands will twitch with heat
You'll feel my breath burn through you and
I'll forget how to behave

I'll have you messing up your hair with frustrated hands
Knowing neither of us will apologize
Just hating me for a split second –
Because *we* are the only way this ends

I know I'm so god damn needy
But it's just because no one else can do it for me
Do you understand this passion I feel for you every time
we get into this zone?

These eyes flash red only with the thought of you being taken away
When my mind is so obsessed I'm losing my senses
Touching myself to our memories
Baby, *please* just come again

So, tell me,
You don't breathe because you need to please me?
Should I remind you of how I can heal you?
You couldn't have known better before
But now you do.
So, come around me and let's just
accelerate and fucking mate.

I Could, But Would I?

I could die and be forsaken

Fortunate as ever and

Condemned to my bones

To have breathed you into my spine

And to have lost you as it breaks.

The Future Has a Past

I understand that after all that time
And all those tries
It was quitting time

And I understand that reason
comes with the seasons
That what you said
Needed saying

And it isn't even
That I regret us ever rhyming
Or beyond that even our fighting

It is because of it
That my future has a past

But I *hate*
That I made you a vow
I can never break

A vow I still owe another to this day

A string of words
I will never be able to share
With the one I truly love most

And it kills me even more
That there never was an end to our story
That I still think of an *us*
When I sincerely don't even want it

After all this time
It just hurts my heart still
To know even I take part
In such *betrayal*

No Love Left to Live

Sometimes you make me sad
So young and always being driven mad
When you look at me like that
Air smashed out of my body
And for a second
No love left to live

Takes a while for me
To stop being mad
And when I'm being honest
It doesn't make it easier
To make you perfect in my head

I figure that's more my thing
Than yours
To be my own worst angel
But greatest devil

I should let go of my vision
And just let you tangle me up in our sheets
Let our silence work this out
So we don't say what isn't there
And find our rest right here.
Just for another day longer.

Preaching's

Remember

You can tell a lot about a man by the way he fucks you

I know

I need to hydrate, but the water I try to inhale turns to sand until my skin is an empty desert.

I know I have been waiting for you my whole life.

Not so long ago, I would flow slowly like honey into the salt of your skin. I want to come in and swim in the golden string you spin. Captivate me, if it is what you will.
Chanting in your thrill, will be my cry of sin.

I know I have been desperate for you all this time.

I feel slightly funny, because the bright sun does not hesitate to burn us as we become strangers from what we know is our purpose. How could we have known, that life can spill just like love does. The air that now flows, is a remnant since you can no longer bare to hold me close.

I know this drought is not endless, but I pray to be reminded of the streams you left in me.

I beg of you, do not be estranged from me. I need your warmth even if I caused your torment. I will give you my all to keep, but whatever it is that is selfish within in me refuses to sleep.

I know I have reason to be afraid so my body contemplates my faith.

You are the sovereign I will trust upon when the sun and the moon lay me down beneath the dirt. I will be placed upon a stand and for my sins I will confess, but for you I will atone when my body no longer inhabits a single bone.

I know I have a heart that rests in that serenity.

We provide each other with a cure.
When you neglect my devotion to you, because you are partly black and mostly blue. Be sure, you will never know anything in life if it is not through my love for you.

I will lie my dignity endlessly at your feet.
You will bow to me even after your last heartbeat.

Fuck I Love You

Who Am I In a Dark Room?

In this dark room
I promise I'm a loyal woman
Faithful to my last bone
That I would let be brazen
If it was for the sake of yours
So please,
Let me drape you under
In the silk that is my care
In the warmth that is my mastery
So, you know
I understand and I see
           You.
Even in this dark room.

Sassy Toys

You better pull that ponytail boy

Or I'll be treating you like a god damn toy

Blue Blood

If you treat me like I'm royal,
I will put you up on a pedestal
And with every touch you'll feel yourself getting high
on this blue blood.

Damned Or Blessed

Tiny ripples of waves flow between us.
Binding us with strings of electricity, sending shocks from my neck to my pumping chest.
The darkness in your eyes should be forbidden in a place so public, and you know exactly why.

Your gaze is undoing the straps tied behind my neck, waiting for the water to flow over my skin.
It intoxicates you.
I want so badly for it to be true because I can feel you longing for me, torn between us two.

What is it about water that makes you want me in this animalistic state?
As soon as the drops slowly drip down my body you stop thinking and just want to ravage me.
I can't fight what you do to me as your exposed touches spark this heat within me, making me feel like the female archetype.

I feel one more unwarranted grip as you force me out and as I walk towards the exit I know exactly what your eyes are fixated on.
I turn around as you make the straps fall down. And though I can't plead for you to own me, your arm around my throat and your hand pressed on my back assure me you do. Protect me while you cover me, my love.

I'm always mesmerized by how something so dirty still makes my need for you feel sane.

But knowing me, damned or blessed I'd do it all again.
And as I feel your pleasure emanating through our movements, I know this won't be the last time we lure the devil into our twisted game.

Him

How the fuck did *I* find him?
And just then,
        Just like that,
                I realize that *he* found me.

Highway Lights

Sometimes I hold your hand
Caressing my thigh
A safe place to land
As highway lights flash by

Time and time again
Bringing to eye
The work of art
That ensues
                      When our bodies collide

Accelerated on Endless Tracks

I'm insecure, but only at times
Overly sensitive, but only when it comes to you.

My face is alluring, my body just is
Yet, I'm shaped heavenly to you.

Many days I'm mad at you at best, but I still demand your understanding
For some reasons, that is something you accept.

When I should give you space, I cling to you as if you're all that makes me breathe.
And yet, your oxygen penetrates through my pores at the expense of your sanity.

Am I trying to make you feel guilty for something you did?
Or did you never really do it at all?
At times, I don't understand the game I'm playing with you either.

So why do you adore me the way you do?
Why do you love me beyond comprehension?
Why the hell do you treat me like there will never be any one else?

Is it so that you love me despite my tantrums, because beyond them I love you more deeply than anyone ever could?
Or do you revel in them because you know you are a necessity to me?

You love me.
You love the woman I am, when I take control and intoxicate you with my instincts.
You love the delicate girl I am, fragile and almost beautifully vulnerable to your every single touch.

There is a harmony to our tensions.
Perhaps that's why we love like we do,
Accelerated, as if there is always another race to win, on a track that is endless.

Story of My Nightlife

I say no to every third drink
because
I'd rather get drunk fucking you sober

Let There Always Be Heat

When there is heat
I am cream and you are flesh
You liquefy me as I drip into your pores
And your love expands into a solid rock
Our voids vanish as we become warm and full – finally.

When our bodies fuck
You are relentless and I am insatiable
I know what you need and my choking throat could prove it
to you down on my knees
You thirst for me and the full body that trademarks me,
wishing you could devour those hips and thighs as they
cover your skin inches thick
What a freak show we oblige to exist

When speed is our desire
You are hunger and I am water
I make you bath in my lips ever so slowly
And your patient anticipation makes my stream a pleasure in
itself
Our thrusts are desperate, so make it to me while you bite my
skin.
I want to feel it sting.

When there is pleasure
I am a beggar and you are air
You bore me so thoroughly that I slip into our promise

And you follow me as I come to the oath of your fingers.
I clench and moan while you unload and groan
We did so good.
Our deepest parts only satisfied when I spill away and we are merged as one.
So, let there always be heat.

My Kind Of 2 A.M.S

It's 2 a.m. and I just got your last text
It's funny how I wait until the moment comes when I don't even know what that means for tonight.

But there's a storm torpedoing through my body and every time I touch myself slowly another wave gushes out of me filling up this room with blazing air.

It's as if I can feel your presence, the buckle of your belt dropping to the floor.
    That sound alone freezes me to my bones.
Your body stepping in bed alongside me, your hands groping my sides and your breath in my ear. *"Celine, are you still awake?"* And I always am.

It's those nights I stay up just to hear you utter a single sentence.
Oh baby, there's this urgency for me to go there, to have you do it right.
To drown and burn in your eyes just to know I'm owned by them.

When we're naked, no barriers or borders.
You unburden me by giving me more.
Promise me another tomorrow.
So, we can love overflowing.

Impatient AF

Just put it in

It's not a sin

Ebbing Excitement

"Stand up straight," he said. "I want you standing still."
So, I did. Anticipation on the full.

Bite marks left on my neck and hands scratching my back.
It hasn't even been touched and I already want to come.

"Look at me. If this is what you want, I need you looking at me."
So, I kept my eyes locked on his.
>   Burning to the ground.

Determined hands went up my sides slipping off the clothing until his lips pulled at mine.
I always forget how much I love the pain.

"Keep looking until it drowns you," he said.
My jeans and panties finally on the ground and his complexion between my thighs. There I go, filling this room with sounds only you will ever know.

So shameless.

Gosh, how do you always know how to take it slow.
So slow.
So, fucking slow until you decide it's okay for me to have it all.

All I can ask myself is if I'm drowning in you or if my own body is just the ecstasy of bliss. All I can hope is that you don't let me go as my body gets ripped in two. And I can only ever blame you.

People are Paradoxes

You are the poison that runs through my blood.
The air that spreads through my lungs.

I run in my lust for the hunt
with a hunger I could never satiate.

The hurt in my limbs that excruciates
Yet the depths of me plead for more.

It's this game I never hesitate to play
when I know it's a loss I could never recover from.

Like fucking pain and pleasure.

You.
You are the paradox of my existence.

Teenage Overwhelming

Gosh I love you.

I love you.

I love you.

I really

Really

Love you.

My Heart Thrives in the Dark

Torment

I am tormented by the sound of the sea, even if silence is
the only thing I see.
Because the waves took away everything, that was ever dear
to me.

So, cold metal froze my hands to the frost of these walls.
And mist surrounds me.
Whirling around like a set of chains made to trespass my
skin and intoxicate my eyes.
And then I am no more than a sliver of moonlight
shinning over the water in a stream to a distant place I
cannot hear.
Adrift and abandoned
by all but me
or
by none but myself.

I'm so Wrong

I wonder would I despair
If there was no light
No warmth to lie in
No heart to hear beat
Surely, I would slowly suffocate!
And be glad to meet my end
What a dark thought it is
But a simplicity of life nonetheless
To be afraid and curious
Of the despair you hope you'll miss

The Final Knot

I'm pushing against a concrete wall
Trying to overcome what I cannot.
The air is shifting as I am drowning
But can I get myself to care? I guess not.

Is this where I fall?
With no ending slot, no final plot?
The darkness surrounds my crowning
And who will be there when I tie my final knot?

No last call.
But at least I've given what I've got.

Love Is Harder Than It's Supposed to Be

On an English pavement
Between a playground and a home
A woman held her child's hand in her own
The woman and child wore matching fur coats
From a Manchester thrift store

When the child picked up five pence off the ground
The mother smiled and told her daughter to keep her find
But the girl answered
"You need it more than I do, *mama*"
So, the mother smiled and tears prickled her eyes
But she answered
"Okay, *mama*"

Now, when I lay myself down to rest
Closing my eyes whilst breathing out
There is a golden vault in my thoughts
It is attached to a million emotional keys
And very rarely do I utter the one word granting entrance

mama.
Today is the first time I have let myself cry for you in twelve years

You birthed me on a 1999 Friday in May
But a wicked game was played
And as the song goes
I bet you never dreamed you'd lose somebody like me
But you did

I rarely want to think about
How your neglect continued our separation
But how was I ever supposed to follow the rules?
When all of you have a second nature
That is painfully born of deception.

Because you and Dad,
You spin fairy tales in your head
They lack no desire or will
                              nor heart or belief
But in the end, you should have known
That dreams based on lies are no more than a fool's paradise
And they inevitably lead those you love most to ruin

And *mama*, now I'm scared I'll do it too

You are all want and emptiness to me
I have so much affection and temper
So much rage and anger
So, I had to build my castles wide enough to centre me
amidst all your ruins

To accept that our paths would be travelled alone
>   that mother and child would not speak
>   that I was abandoned, and daughter of no one
>   that I was alone in defending you
>   that you would not help me see
the love you have for me

See *mama,* for so long I could not cry

But I cannot lay blame to you alone
When it is mostly through the cruel way of the world
That women have to move on and leave behind
>   ***to sacrifice***
to become someone

So, I choose to believe that motherhood
Requires the greatest forgiveness
Because our family is breaking at the seams
And life is nothing like we pictured it

But in me, you instilled part of my strength and wit.
Part of my denial and numbness – greed and destruction.

But mostly my fight, *mama*

The sad thing – the heart-breaking thing
Is just that your fight will be losing me
>   and mine will be missing out on you

In the end – we will have just spent a lifetime getting over
the trauma we caused each other.
But since you believe in God
And I believe in my own fairy tales now
We will just need to have faith
That in the end
We find out who we want to be
So, Mother and Daughter can move on to become someone

Right, *mama?*

Desperation For Evermore

Sit with me by the setting sun
It will blind us eventually
So, we can forget all that is terrible
Just until the screams of the world pierce through
And we are left to the endless inevitable
                            Desperation – For evermore

Lord, Do I?

Sometimes I see God
Vivid in clear shattered glass

Sometimes I see God
Ferocious in silent devastation

Sometimes I see God
Imperfect in birth of the universe

Sometimes I fear I see God
       and
Sometimes I fear I do not

Sorrow

Sorrow finds young girls
Young girls, just like me
And I had short curls and a pink two piece

But sorrow,
I don't want him touching me
I don't want him on me or all over me

Sorrow,
Will the walls of this tent keep my secrets?

Sorrow,
Sweet, sweet sorrow,
It seems I have no say
Not in who keeps me
Or who corners me

So, sorrow,
I let him enter me – giggling afraid
And wreckage comes over me

Sorrow, you did not help me
I wanted everyone to see and to know
But alas I was already too good at hiding me

So now
In silence I will scream
And in rain I will rally
But in love I will quiver

Because once touched is always marked
And this one will scorch, sear and scorn

Speak Angel to Me

I think I feel weak
For I am only strong
To know you are with me

I think I don't forge on
For I only go forward
To know you will be with me

I fear my heart burns for just one purpose
For I only feel ecstasy in my peace
To know you are to stay with me

I am driven out of control by such delirium
For I have unfailingly been so strong
Until I was lost to the world, diminished to nothing but a
sole force of colossal love for you.
So unaware that over time this virtue kept me from crumbling
beneath the pain and the agony.

So, if this is all I can be in life
I beg you see the value in my wings
Show me the appreciation you have for my halo
And let your lips speak angel to me
Enlighten me so I know I am meant for this

Irrevocable Strength

Behind the Bars of My Mind.

I keep begging

praying for help

S a l v a t i o n

But it's all in vain

Because if I say it any louder

No one is going to save me from myself

Or the dissolution I love to feel

So, I just need you to stand by me

And come over me

And fuck me like you do

Because you can't hurt me

And what I became

Is a monster to myself?

And I'm not ashamed that I made myself a prisoner addicted to a life that only exists behind the bars of my mind.

Honestly,

When I look into my eyes I bring heaven to my life.

I Still Don't Remember Being Truly Broken

I never know if I want to find my strength in childish crying
In victimized hiding
In eerily vacant feminine eyes
Or alternate universes in my mind

I just know I don't need anyone to dry my eyes
Might be an absolute fucking train wreck
But still don't remember ever being truly broken

I just need to learn
Not to take the anger I have
For all you moronic maniacs out on myself

I can only fill all my hunger with bitterness for so long
Before I start to spew venom
and burst at the seams

Watch Me

Watch me burn – I am the fire that will devastate

Watch me drown – I am the water that is holy

Watch me choke – I am the air that you breathe

Watch me come alive – I am undone by you thunder

Make Me

Breath me in your story
The whispers soothing my neck
The words sliding down my spine
Allow our love to lust

Make me forget
Let me trust
Settle me under
Enclose my deliverance

Help me slip below the surface
Pull me underneath in a devastating silence
Through the bend of the water watch the burning stars and
the bowing mountains

Make me fire
Let me burn
Settle me in
Enclose me in your ashes

From there let new creation begin
from that which is scattered
So, we will worship what is born anew
And be lifted high on the wind that soars
A hundred billion times in pursuit of what can never be

Lips

I lie waiting for you in our bed
Naked
Soft blankets against my skin
Just waiting for you to find me covered in nude sin

When your eyes meet my shoulders
Making the blanket drop
Breasts heave slowly

Nipples want to be met with your pride
Thighs are spread and so are lips
I am open to you as you wish

So, do I make you proud when I show myself to you, all ready and yours to be taken?
Good
because I have been wet since the raining dawn of day

More Admiration

It's just that once I'm in a room with you
                in *our bed,*
I feel so beautiful because I'm a part of you
And beauty may be superficial, but it can perplex a nation
And I don't need the awe of a dominion because it
dissolves in the wake of your admiration
And somehow, I just want it more
                so much more.

Get Me Acquainted

Thinking of you and I

Makes my pussy clench

Close my eyes as I am

Just to have them roll back in sync with my head and back

Fuck it

I promise I will try so hard

Just get me acquainted

I *need* to sex all night. So much desperation

What did you do to me?

Making my fantasies reality

Locked inside this fantasia

Where I see in you

Like nobody does.

When you show me all because I take you as you are.

I'm Such a Power Piece

Do you get that feeling from morning to evening?
Who can turn you on?
Imagine your silhouette.
Do you see your hands, the length of your fingers?
They can.
Feel the blood rushing through your body.
Do you want it bad enough?
To know
to whom you belong?
Confine yourself and feel the control take over.
It's all your own.
Make it your show.
Put in work.
Push it to the limit but take your time.
No point in skipping over what you deserve.
You can come in discretion.

But

In my craze I have bills flying all over me.
Sticking to the sweat of my own heat.
Might even tip myself for the sounds coming out of my lips.
And the higher I start climbing the more I want to keep gripping.
Might do it anyway just to taste the goodness that is myself.
And the rawer I get the more I give myself credit.
Might just get a videographer to lock down the faces I

make – nothing more angelic than your own self-made satisfaction.
And the bills just keep coming.
This ambiance got me heightened.
And from morning to evening
I'll be making money.

So now you know
Who you belong to.
My love is none other
Than fucking mine.

I Will

I'll take heed on your hunt
                and bide my time
I'll obey your hands
                as they twist me inside out
I'll sit indefensibly as your arch is shot
                to the ploy of my back
So unequivocally
                You pierce me through.

Somebody to Love

We were seventeen then
I am a woman now
But I remember our faces
Wide-eyed and blemished
So much that was still unknown
When a girlish heart first learns to love a boy
And you are still my all and more

We were seventeen then
You are a man now
But I remember how we started
Bursting smiles and gentle talks
So much that we wanted to learn
When a boy first learns to gently touch a girl
And I am still the one you constantly desire

We find our lives spilling out over this bedroom floor
Still looking for somebody to love
Clinging together every time sundown covers us
We taught each other all and yet there is so much more.
Just as long as our hearts keep lighting up like when we
were seventeen
                Chasing that freedom you and I know exists
                      only right here.

Bring My Name Back to Life

Have you ever needed a vessel
To carry you out of the fickle waters
And put your body afloat on that which is cold?

Have you ever been hanging by a thread
But walked the soil with grace still
And cast your chin forward when you have no course to navigate?

Have you ever been shattered?
With no spirit left in your bones
And looked at yourself with love through your eyes?

You have raised that broken self from the grounds and waters
Breath by breath awakening a name back to life
So that you have become a vessel ever flowing.

What Happens in Eternity?

"With every heartbeat I have left
I will love you far longer than death"

-

It is the first promise we made
And I vow to keep it closest to my heart
For it is all I believe in

My Love

How do I breathe in?
And for the first time,
I am shocked
For the air is pure.

And so I wonder
At the top of this great mountain
How it is
That I was mended

As my hands held tight
To my own frail heart
I climbed and I climbed

So somehow
I became so much more
Than a daughter of no one
And everyone in between

And my eyes met above me
My reflection in the darkness
So, they spoke with grace abound
"My love, you have found peace.
So now, you leap forth and live so you will soar".

This Is Where the Story Ends

My loves,
For now,
This is where the story ends.
As for now,
I have given you most of me.

But at the edge of nights,
which is when I imagine you
reading my precious tiny tales,
know in the worst of times
there will always be whimsical places to escape to.

I hope my story was one of them for you.

But remember, you can always make your own.

Thank you, deeply.

Yours,
Celine Maria

www.ingramcontent.com/pod-product-compliance
Lightning Source LLC
LaVergne TN
LVHW061417290125
802306LV00013B/324